LIFE IN THE SUPERNATURAL
Christ's Ministry Through Us!

Retreat/Group Companion
WORKBOOK
RICHARD T. CASE

*To my wife, Linda,
who is always noticing, experiencing and sharing
the supernatural things of God in our everyday life.
She is a prayer warrior and as we seek God's resolutions
to life issues and His revelation of new understanding of the Covenant life,
Linda gets excited about the supernatural activity of God.
She always expects it and has been a wonderful encouragement
to stay with receiving God's best for us, which is always beyond us and our
natural abilities–He loves to do wondrous works.
She is truly an inspiration and a privilege
to walk together in the Supernatural.*

Acknowledgments

We wish to thank all of the leaders of our **Ministry: Living Waters—ABIDE Ministries!** These leaders have learned what it means to live in the Supernatural and now are giving this away to others—who are learning to live in the supernatural; and it is exponentially multiplying. Thank you all:

These leaders are:

Jake and Mary Beckel
Joe and Leigh Bogar
Rich and Janet Cocchiaro
Larry and Sherry Collet
Scott and Kristen Cornell
David and Melissa Dunkel
Tom and Susanne Ewing
Rick and Kelly Ferris
Joel and Christina Gunn
Scott and Terry Hitchcock
Chris and Jaclyn Hoover
Rick and Nancy Hoover
Tad and Monica Jones
Ed and Becky Kobel
Don and Rachelle Light
Chris and Heidi May
Terry and Josephine Noetzel
Steve and Carolyn Van Ooteghem
Preston and Lynda Pitts
Dan and Kathy Rocconi
Bob and Keri Rockwell
John and Michelle Santaferraro
Allyson and Denny Weinberg
Neal and Kathy Weisenburger

LIFE IN THE SUPERNATURAL: COMPANION WORKBOOK
PUBLISHED BY LIVING WATERS—ABIDE MINISTRIES
7615 Lemon Gulch Way
Castle Rock, CO 80108

Unless otherwise noted, all Scripture quotations are from the ESV® Bible (The Holy Bible, English Standard Version®), copyright © 2001 by Crossway Bibles, a publishing ministry of Good News Publishers. Used by permission. All rights reserved.

ISBN: 978-1-7360588-3-1
Copyright © 2024 by Richard T. Case.

All rights reserved. No part of this publication may be reproduced, distributed or transmitted in any form or by any means, including photocopying, recording, or other electronic or mechanical methods, without the prior written permission of the publisher.

Publisher's Cataloging-in-Publication data

Printed in the United States of America 2024 — 2nd ed

TABLE OF CONTENTS

Introduction 1

Lesson One:
Regarding the Supernatural:
We Have Questions For Jesus, and Jesus Has Questions For Us. 4

Lesson Two:
What Authority Brings About the Supernatural?. 18

Lesson Three:
What are the Keys to Experiencing the Supernatural? 28

Lesson Four:
How Do We Limit His Supernatural Work?. 38

Lesson Five:
What Is Important If We Are to Experience the Supernatural?. 54

Lesson Six:
As We Experience the Supernatural, We Also Are Called to Help Others
Experience the Supernatural 66

LIFE IN THE SUPERNATURAL
Christ's Ministry Through Us!

INTRODUCTION

INTRODUCTION

Read Hebrews 2:1-4:

Warning Against Neglecting Salvation
² Therefore we must pay much closer attention to what we have heard, lest we drift away from it. ² For since the message declared by angels proved to be reliable, and every transgression or disobedience received a just retribution, ³ how shall we escape if we neglect such a great salvation? It was declared at first by the Lord, and it was attested to us by those who heard,⁴ while God also bore witness by signs and wonders and various miracles and by gifts of the Holy Spirit distributed according to his will.

What does God say about our great salvation? What is salvation?

_____
_____
_____
_____
_____
_____
_____

If you'd like to know more about
Abide Ministries,
please see our pages
at the back of the workbook

INTRODUCTION

What is the reason, the purpose for the supernatural (the miraculous)?

_____
_____
_____
_____
_____
_____
_____

> **Read John 14:12-14:**
>
> [12] "Truly, truly, I say to you, whoever believes in me will also do the works that I do; and greater works than these will he do, because I am going to the Father. [13] Whatever you ask in my name, this I will do, that the Father may be glorified in the Son. [14] If you ask me[a] anything in my name, I will do it.

What does God say regarding our participation in these miracles? Who is to be included in this?

_____
_____
_____
_____
_____

LESSON 1:
REGARDING THE SUPERNATURAL:
WE HAVE QUESTIONS FOR JESUS, AND JESUS HAS QUESTIONS FOR US

As we start to understand the supernatural, we're going to engage in an interesting exercise that will help clarify these two points:

1. What are our legitimate, heart-felt questions that we wonder about with regard to this area of the supernatural?

2. Interestingly enough, Jesus has questions right back to us. He asks, "Where are we regarding the truth of the supernatural?"

Let's begin with our questions to Jesus:

WHAT ARE OUR QUESTIONS TO JESUS?

For each of the following verses, write out what the questions were to Jesus about the supernatural (which are still our questions today):

> **Read Matthew 8:2:**
>
> 2 And behold, a leper[a] came to him and knelt before him, saying, "Lord, if you will, you can make me clean."

_____
_____
_____
_____
_____
_____
_____

LESSON 1:
REGARDING THE SUPERNATURAL:
WE HAVE QUESTIONS FOR JESUS, AND JESUS HAS QUESTIONS FOR US

Read Matthew 12:10:

¹⁰ And a man was there with a withered hand. And they asked him, "Is it lawful to heal on the Sabbath?"— so that they might accuse him.

_____
_____
_____
_____
_____

Read Matthew 14:28:

²⁸ And Peter answered him, "Lord, if it is you, command me to come to you on the water."

_____
_____
_____
_____
_____

Read Mark 5:35:

³⁵ While he was still speaking, there came from the ruler's house some who said, "Your daughter is dead. Why trouble the Teacher any further?"

_____
_____
_____
_____
_____

LESSON 1:
REGARDING THE SUPERNATURAL:
WE HAVE QUESTIONS FOR JESUS, AND JESUS HAS QUESTIONS FOR US

> **Read Mark 9:22:**
>
> ²² And it has often cast him into fire and into water, to destroy him. But if you can do anything, have compassion on us and help us."

_____
_____
_____
_____
_____

These are real and honest, legitimate questions. Well, interestingly enough, Jesus asks us questions right back.

Now, let's consider those questions Jesus might have for us.

WHAT ARE JESUS' QUESTIONS TO US?

> **Read Matthew 8:26:**
>
> ²⁶ And he said to them, "Why are you afraid, O you of little faith?" Then he rose and rebuked the winds and the sea, and there was a great calm.

_____
_____
_____
_____
_____

LESSON 1:
REGARDING THE SUPERNATURAL:
WE HAVE QUESTIONS FOR JESUS, AND JESUS HAS QUESTIONS FOR US

Read Matthew 9:28:

28 When he entered the house, the blind men came to him, and Jesus said to them, "Do you believe that I am able to do this?" They said to him, "Yes, Lord."

_____
_____
_____
_____

Read Matthew 20:32:

32 And stopping, Jesus called them and said, "What do you want me to do for you?"

_____
_____
_____
_____

Read Mark 3:4:

4 And he said to them, "Is it lawful on the Sabbath to do good or to do harm, to save life or to kill?" But they were silent.

_____
_____
_____
_____

LESSON 1:
REGARDING THE SUPERNATURAL:
WE HAVE QUESTIONS FOR JESUS, AND JESUS HAS QUESTIONS FOR US

Read Mark 5:30:

30 And Jesus, perceiving in himself that power had gone out from him, immediately turned about in the crowd and said, "Who touched my garments?"

Read Mark 6:38:

38 And he said to them, "How many loaves do you have? Go and see." And when they had found out, they said, "Five, and two fish."

Read Mark 8:12:

12 And he sighed deeply in his spirit and said, "Why does this generation seek a sign? Truly, I say to you, no sign will be given to this generation."

LESSON 1:
REGARDING THE SUPERNATURAL:
WE HAVE QUESTIONS FOR JESUS, AND JESUS HAS QUESTIONS FOR US

Read John 5:6:

6 When Jesus saw him lying there and knew that he had already been there a long time, he said to him, "Do you want to be healed?"

_____
_____
_____
_____

Read John 9:35:

35 Jesus heard that they had cast him out, and having found him he said, "Do you believe in the Son of Man?"[a]

_____
_____
_____
_____

Read John 11:40:

40 Jesus said to her, "Did I not tell you that if you believed you would see the glory of God?"

_____
_____
_____
_____

LESSON 1:
REGARDING THE SUPERNATURAL:
WE HAVE QUESTIONS FOR JESUS, AND JESUS HAS QUESTIONS FOR US

> **Read Matthew 8:5-9:**
>
> The Faith of a Centurion
> [5] When he had entered Capernaum, a centurion came forward to him, appealing to him, [6] "Lord, my servant is lying paralyzed at home, suffering terribly." [7] And he said to him, "I will come and heal him." [8] But the centurion replied, "Lord, I am not worthy to have you come under my roof, but only say the word, and my servant will be healed. [9] For I too am a man under authority, with soldiers under me. And I say to one, 'Go,' and he goes, and to another, 'Come,' and he comes, and to my servant,[a] 'Do this,' and he does it."

What did the Centurion understand regarding how the supernatural works? On what basis does this work? Why?

_____
_____
_____
_____
_____

LESSON 1:
REGARDING THE SUPERNATURAL:
WE HAVE QUESTIONS FOR JESUS, AND JESUS HAS QUESTIONS FOR US

> **Read Matthew 12:9-14:**
>
> A Man with a Withered Hand
> ⁹ He went on from there and entered their synagogue. ¹⁰ And a man was there with a withered hand. And they asked him, "Is it lawful to heal on the Sabbath?"—so that they might accuse him. ¹¹ He said to them, "Which one of you who has a sheep, if it falls into a pit on the Sabbath, will not take hold of it and lift it out? ¹² Of how much more value is a man than a sheep! So it is lawful to do good on the Sabbath." ¹³ Then he said to the man, "Stretch out your hand." And the man stretched it out, and it was restored, healthy like the other. ¹⁴ But the Pharisees went out and conspired against him, how to destroy him.

What is the key to how we look at the supernatural? How does Christ want us to think about issues and problems we have?

_____
_____
_____
_____
_____

LESSON 1:
REGARDING THE SUPERNATURAL:
WE HAVE QUESTIONS FOR JESUS, AND JESUS HAS QUESTIONS FOR US

> **Read Matthew 13:53-54:**
>
> Jesus Rejected at Nazareth
> 53 And when Jesus had finished these parables, he went away from there, 54 and coming to his hometown he taught them in their synagogue, so that they were astonished, and said, "Where did this man get this wisdom and these mighty works?

How does wisdom and receiving truth play into experiencing the supernatural? Why?

_____
_____
_____
_____
_____

> **Read Mark 7:33-37:**
>
> 33 And taking him aside from the crowd privately, he put his fingers into his ears, and after spitting touched his tongue. 34 And looking up to heaven, he sighed and said to him, "Ephphatha," that is, "Be opened." 35 And his ears were opened, his tongue was released, and he spoke plainly. 36 And Jesus[a] charged them to tell no one. But the more he charged them, the more zealously they proclaimed it. 37 And they were astonished beyond measure, saying, "He has done all things well. He even makes the deaf hear and the mute speak."

How did those experiencing the miraculous describe the nature of the miraculous? What does this mean?

_____
_____
_____
_____
_____

LESSON 1:
REGARDING THE SUPERNATURAL:
WE HAVE QUESTIONS FOR JESUS, AND JESUS HAS QUESTIONS FOR US

> **Read Luke 9:1:**
>
> Jesus Sends Out the Twelve Apostles
> [9] And he called the twelve together and gave them power and authority over all demons and to cure diseases,

To whom did He give His supernatural power to exercise in their lives? Why is this important?

_____
_____
_____
_____
_____

> **Read Luke 17:11-14:**
>
> Jesus Cleanses Ten Lepers
> [11] On the way to Jerusalem he was passing along between Samaria and Galilee. [12] And as he entered a village, he was met by ten lepers,[a] who stood at a distance [13] and lifted up their voices, saying, "Jesus, Master, have mercy on us." [14] When he saw them he said to them, "Go and show yourselves to the priests." And as they went, they were cleansed.

What was required for those with leprosy to experience the supernatural? Why is this important?

_____
_____
_____
_____
_____

LESSON 1:
REGARDING THE SUPERNATURAL:
WE HAVE QUESTIONS FOR JESUS, AND JESUS HAS QUESTIONS FOR US

Read John 2:1-11:

The Wedding at Cana

2 On the third day there was a wedding at Cana in Galilee, and the mother of Jesus was there. 2 Jesus also was invited to the wedding with his disciples. 3 When the wine ran out, the mother of Jesus said to him, "They have no wine." 4 And Jesus said to her, "Woman, what does this have to do with me? My hour has not yet come." 5 His mother said to the servants, "Do whatever he tells you."

6 Now there were six stone water jars there for the Jewish rites of purification, each holding twenty or thirty gallons.[a] 7 Jesus said to the servants, "Fill the jars with water." And they filled them up to the brim. 8 And he said to them, "Now draw some out and take it to the master of the feast." So they took it. 9 When the master of the feast tasted the water now become wine, and did not know where it came from (though the servants who had drawn the water knew), the master of the feast called the bridegroom 10 and said to him, "Everyone serves the good wine first, and when people have drunk freely, then the poor wine. But you have kept the good wine until now." 11 This, the first of his signs, Jesus did at Cana in Galilee, and manifested his glory. And his disciples believed in him.

How did this miracle happen? What did Jesus do to perform this miracle? Why is this important for us?

_____
_____
_____
_____
_____

LESSON 1:
REGARDING THE SUPERNATURAL:
WE HAVE QUESTIONS FOR JESUS, AND JESUS HAS QUESTIONS FOR US

> **Read John 6:15-21:**
>
> [15] Perceiving then that they were about to come and take him by force to make him king, Jesus withdrew again to the mountain by himself.
>
> Jesus Walks on Water
> [16] When evening came, his disciples went down to the sea, [17] got into a boat, and started across the sea to Capernaum. It was now dark, and Jesus had not yet come to them. [18] The sea became rough because a strong wind was blowing. [19] When they had rowed about three or four miles,[a] they saw Jesus walking on the sea and coming near the boat, and they were frightened. [20] But he said to them, "It is I; do not be afraid."[21] Then they were glad to take him into the boat, and immediately the boat was at the land to which they were going.

What does this story demonstrate God has power/authority over? Why is this important to us?

_____
_____
_____
_____
_____

LESSON 1:
REGARDING THE SUPERNATURAL:
WE HAVE QUESTIONS FOR JESUS, AND JESUS HAS QUESTIONS FOR US

> **Read John 11:25-26:**
>
> [25] Jesus said to her, "I am the resurrection and the life.[a] Whoever believes in me, though he die, yet shall he live, [26] and everyone who lives and believes in me shall never die. Do you believe this?"

What does Christ speak to about the source of the supernatural? Why is this important to us?

_____
_____
_____
_____
_____

LESSON 2:
WHAT AUTHORITY BRINGS ABOUT THE SUPERNATURAL?

We're in session two of our study on life in the supernatural. As we look at the supernatural, He wants us to remember that He is to bear witness to innumerable miracles in our everyday life. John, too, in his Book of John, wrote that God invites us to miracles. As we learned in Session One, He basically asks us if we are willing to believe in the supernatural and understand what that looks like? The key we must understand is that this is about authority. His supernatural is based upon His authority, which is superior to our everyday circumstances. And He wants to have that play out in our everyday life so that His authority begins to deliver supernatural answers to our everyday issues. In this session, we will look at the important features of what this authority is over and what it is not over.

UNDERSTANDING IMPORTANT FEATURES OF HIS AUTHORITY:

In each of these sets of verses, write out what He has authority over:

> **Matthew 8:3; 5-7, 13; 14; 16-17; 23-27; 28-34:**
>
> 3 And Jesus[a] stretched out his hand and touched him, saying, "I will; be clean." And immediately his leprosy was cleansed.
>
> 5 When he had entered Capernaum, a centurion came forward to him, appealing to him, 6 "Lord, my servant is lying paralyzed at home, suffering terribly." 7 And he said to him, "I will come and heal him."
>
> 13 And to the centurion Jesus said, "Go; let it be done for you as you have believed." And the servant was healed at that very moment.
>
> 14 And when Jesus entered Peter's house, he saw his mother-in-law lying sick with a fever.

LESSON 2:
WHAT AUTHORITY BRINGS ABOUT THE SUPERNATURAL?

[16] That evening they brought to him many who were oppressed by demons, and he cast out the spirits with a word and healed all who were sick. [17] This was to fulfill what was spoken by the prophet Isaiah: "He took our illnesses and bore our diseases."

[23] And when he got into the boat, his disciples followed him. [24] And behold, there arose a great storm on the sea, so that the boat was being swamped by the waves; but he was asleep. [25] And they went and woke him, saying, "Save us, Lord; we are perishing." [26] And he said to them, "Why are you afraid, O you of little faith?" Then he rose and rebuked the winds and the sea, and there was a great calm. [27] And the men marveled, saying, "What sort of man is this, that even winds and sea obey him?"

Jesus Heals Two Men with Demons
[28] And when he came to the other side, to the country of the Gadarenes,[a] two demon-possessed[b] men met him, coming out of the tombs, so fierce that no one could pass that way. [29] And behold, they cried out, "What have you to do with us, O Son of God? Have you come here to torment us before the time?" [30] Now a herd of many pigs was feeding at some distance from them. [31] And the demons begged him, saying, "If you cast us out, send us away into the herd of pigs." [32] And he said to them, "Go." So they came out and went into the pigs, and behold, the whole herd rushed down the steep bank into the sea and drowned in the waters. [33] The herdsmen fled, and going into the city they told everything, especially what had happened to the demon-possessed men. [34] And behold, all the city came out to meet Jesus, and when they saw him, they begged him to leave their region.

_____
_____
_____
_____
_____

LESSON 2:
WHAT AUTHORITY BRINGS ABOUT THE SUPERNATURAL?

Matthew 10:1-15:

The Twelve Apostles
10 And he called to him his twelve disciples and gave them authority over unclean spirits, to cast them out, and to heal every disease and every affliction. ² The names of the twelve apostles are these: first, Simon, who is called Peter, and Andrew his brother; James the son of Zebedee, and John his brother; ³ Philip and Bartholomew; Thomas and Matthew the tax collector; James the son of Alphaeus, and Thaddaeus;[a] ⁴ Simon the Zealot,[b] and Judas Iscariot, who betrayed him.

Jesus Sends Out the Twelve Apostles
⁵ These twelve Jesus sent out, instructing them, "Go nowhere among the Gentiles and enter no town of the Samaritans, ⁶ but go rather to the lost sheep of the house of Israel. ⁷ And proclaim as you go, saying, 'The kingdom of heaven is at hand.'[c] ⁸ Heal the sick, raise the dead, cleanse lepers,[d] cast out demons. You received without paying; give without pay. ⁹ Acquire no gold or silver or copper for your belts, ¹⁰ no bag for your journey, or two tunics[e] or sandals or a staff, for the laborer deserves his food. ¹¹ And whatever town or village you enter, find out who is worthy in it and stay there until you depart. ¹² As you enter the house, greet it.¹³ And if the house is worthy, let your peace come upon it, but if it is not worthy, let your peace return to you. ¹⁴ And if anyone will not receive you or listen to your words, shake off the dust from your feet when you leave that house or town. ¹⁵ Truly, I say to you, it will be more bearable on the day of judgment for the land of Sodom and Gomorrah than for that town.

_____
_____
_____
_____
_____

LESSON 2:
WHAT AUTHORITY BRINGS ABOUT THE SUPERNATURAL?

Luke 8:22-56:

Jesus Calms a Storm

22 One day he got into a boat with his disciples, and he said to them, "Let us go across to the other side of the lake." So they set out, 23 and as they sailed he fell asleep. And a windstorm came down on the lake, and they were filling with water and were in danger. 24 And they went and woke him, saying, "Master, Master, we are perishing!" And he awoke and rebuked the wind and the raging waves, and they ceased, and there was a calm. 25 He said to them, "Where is your faith?" And they were afraid, and they marveled, saying to one another, "Who then is this, that he commands even winds and water, and they obey him?"

Jesus Heals a Man with a Demon

26 Then they sailed to the country of the Gerasenes,[a] which is opposite Galilee. 27 When Jesus[b] had stepped out on land, there met him a man from the city who had demons. For a long time he had worn no clothes, and he had not lived in a house but among the tombs. 28 When he saw Jesus, he cried out and fell down before him and said with a loud voice, "What have you to do with me, Jesus, Son of the Most High God? I beg you, do not torment me." 29 For he had commanded the unclean spirit to come out of the man. (For many a time it had seized him. He was kept under guard and bound with chains and shackles, but he would break the bonds and be driven by the demon into the desert.) 30 Jesus then asked him, "What is your name?" And he said, "Legion," for many demons had entered him. 31 And they begged him not to command them to depart into the abyss. 32 Now a large herd of pigs was feeding there on the hillside, and they begged him to let them enter these. So he gave them permission. 33 Then the demons came out of the man and entered the pigs, and the herd rushed down the steep bank into the lake and drowned.

34 When the herdsmen saw what had happened, they fled and told it in the city and in the country. 35 Then people went out to see what had happened, and they came to Jesus and found the man from whom the demons had gone, sitting at the feet of Jesus, clothed and in his right mind, and they were afraid. 36 And those who had seen it told them how the demon-possessed[c] man had been healed. 37 Then all the people of the surrounding country of the Gerasenes asked him to depart from them, for they were seized with great fear. So he got into the boat and returned. 38 The man from whom the demons had gone begged that he might be with him, but Jesus sent him away, saying, 39 "Return to your home, and declare how much God has done for you." And he went away, proclaiming throughout the whole city how much Jesus had done for him.

LESSON 2:
WHAT AUTHORITY BRINGS ABOUT THE SUPERNATURAL?

Jesus Heals a Woman and Jairus's Daughter

[40] Now when Jesus returned, the crowd welcomed him, for they were all waiting for him. [41] And there came a man named Jairus, who was a ruler of the synagogue. And falling at Jesus' feet, he implored him to come to his house, [42] for he had an only daughter, about twelve years of age, and she was dying.

As Jesus went, the people pressed around him. [43] And there was a woman who had had a discharge of blood for twelve years, and though she had spent all her living on physicians,[d] she could not be healed by anyone. [44] She came up behind him and touched the fringe of his garment, and immediately her discharge of blood ceased. [45] And Jesus said, "Who was it that touched me?" When all denied it, Peter[e] said, "Master, the crowds surround you and are pressing in on you!" [46] But Jesus said, "Someone touched me, for I perceive that power has gone out from me." [47] And when the woman saw that she was not hidden, she came trembling, and falling down before him declared in the presence of all the people why she had touched him, and how she had been immediately healed. [48] And he said to her, "Daughter, your faith has made you well; go in peace."

[49] While he was still speaking, someone from the ruler's house came and said, "Your daughter is dead; do not trouble the Teacher anymore." [50] But Jesus on hearing this answered him, "Do not fear; only believe, and she will be well." [51] And when he came to the house, he allowed no one to enter with him, except Peter and John and James, and the father and mother of the child. [52] And all were weeping and mourning for her, but he said, "Do not weep, for she is not dead but sleeping." [53] And they laughed at him, knowing that she was dead. [54] But taking her by the hand he called, saying, "Child, arise." [55] And her spirit returned, and she got up at once. And he directed that something should be given her to eat. [56] And her parents were amazed, but he charged them to tell no one what had happened.

LESSON 2:
WHAT AUTHORITY BRINGS ABOUT THE SUPERNATURAL?

Here, He has authority over nature, demons, death (through resurrection), long-term infirmity, sickness—all issues that were subordinate to His power.

As we consider all this, there is an important issue to understand. He has authority over all these various things in our life. But there is something that He does not take authority over. What do you think this is and why?

_____
_____
_____
_____
_____

Read Mark 9:38-41:

Anyone Not Against Us Is for Us

38 John said to him, "Teacher, we saw someone casting out demons in your name,[a] and we tried to stop him, because he was not following us." 39 But Jesus said, "Do not stop him, for no one who does a mighty work in my name will be able soon afterward to speak evil of me. 40 For the one who is not against us is for us. 41 For truly, I say to you, whoever gives you a cup of water to drink because you belong to Christ will by no means lose his reward.

What is the main point of this story regarding experiencing the supernatural? Why is this so significant?

_____
_____
_____
_____
_____

LESSON 2:
WHAT AUTHORITY BRINGS ABOUT THE SUPERNATURAL?

Read John 2:11:

[11] This, the first of his signs, Jesus did at Cana in Galilee, and manifested his glory. And his disciples believed in him.

In His first miracle, what did Jesus say was the purpose behind it? Why?

_____
_____
_____
_____

Read John 5:30-47:

Witnesses to Jesus

[30] "I can do nothing on my own. As I hear, I judge, and my judgment is just, because I seek not my own will but the will of him who sent me. [31] If I alone bear witness about myself, my testimony is not true. [32] There is another who bears witness about me, and I know that the testimony that he bears about me is true. [33] You sent to John, and he has borne witness to the truth. [34] Not that the testimony that I receive is from man, but I say these things so that you may be saved. [35] He was a burning and shining lamp, and you were willing to rejoice for a while in his light. [36] But the testimony that I have is greater than that of John. For the works that the Father has given me to accomplish, the very works that I am doing, bear witness about me that the Father has sent me. [37] And the Father who sent me has himself borne witness about me. His voice you have never heard, his form you have never seen, [38] and you do not have his word abiding in you, for you do not believe the one whom he has sent. [39] You search the Scriptures because you think that in them you have eternal life; and it is they that bear witness about me, [40] yet you refuse to come to me that you may have life. [41] I do not receive glory from people. [42] But I know that you do not have the

LESSON 2:
WHAT AUTHORITY BRINGS ABOUT THE SUPERNATURAL?

> love of God within you. ⁴³ I have come in my Father's name, and you do not receive me. If another comes in his own name, you will receive him. ⁴⁴ How can you believe, when you receive glory from one another and do not seek the glory that comes from the only God? ⁴⁵ Do not think that I will accuse you to the Father. There is one who accuses you: Moses, on whom you have set your hope. ⁴⁶ For if you believed Moses, you would believe me; for he wrote of me. ⁴⁷ But if you do not believe his writings, how will you believe my words?"

In this argument that Jesus sets forth, what does Jesus state as the reason for the supernatural? Why is this so important to learn?

_____
_____
_____
_____
_____

LESSON 2:
WHAT AUTHORITY BRINGS ABOUT THE SUPERNATURAL?

> **Read John 8:48-59:**
>
> Before Abraham Was, I Am
>
> [48] The Jews answered him, "Are we not right in saying that you are a Samaritan and have a demon?" [49] Jesus answered, "I do not have a demon, but I honor my Father, and you dishonor me. [50] Yet I do not seek my own glory; there is One who seeks it, and he is the judge. [51] Truly, truly, I say to you, if anyone keeps my word, he will never see death." [52] The Jews said to him, "Now we know that you have a demon! Abraham died, as did the prophets, yet you say, 'If anyone keeps my word, he will never taste death.' [53] Are you greater than our father Abraham, who died? And the prophets died! Who do you make yourself out to be?" [54] Jesus answered, "If I glorify myself, my glory is nothing. It is my Father who glorifies me, of whom you say, 'He is our God.'[a] [55] But you have not known him. I know him. If I were to say that I do not know him, I would be a liar like you, but I do know him and I keep his word. [56] Your father Abraham rejoiced that he would see my day. He saw it and was glad." [57] So the Jews said to him, "You are not yet fifty years old, and have you seen Abraham?"[b] [58] Jesus said to them, "Truly, truly, I say to you, before Abraham was, I am." [59] So they picked up stones to throw at him, but Jesus hid himself and went out of the temple.

What point does Jesus make about His nature? If we are to believe this, what must we experience, and what does it do to reinforce who He is and what His nature is?

_____
_____
_____
_____
_____

LESSON 2:
WHAT AUTHORITY BRINGS ABOUT THE SUPERNATURAL?

> **Read John 11:4; 40-42:**
>
> ⁴ But when Jesus heard it he said, "This illness does not lead to death. It is for the glory of God, so that the Son of God may be glorified through it."
>
> ⁴⁰ Jesus said to her, "Did I not tell you that if you believed you would see the glory of God?" ⁴¹ So they took away the stone. And Jesus lifted up his eyes and said, "Father, I thank you that you have heard me. ⁴² I knew that you always hear me, but I said this on account of the people standing around, that they may believe that you sent me."

What did Christ say was the purpose of this sickness and then the purpose of the miracle that He performs? Why is this important to our understanding of the purpose of Him doing miracles in our lives?

_____
_____
_____
_____
_____

LESSON 3:
WHAT ARE THE KEYS TO EXPERIENCING THE SUPERNATURAL?

The life of the supernatural is to understand that God wants to bear witness with miracles, miracles, miracles; and not neglect so great a salvation. So that's what we're trying to understand. John tells us that he wrote about the miracles so that we might believe it and begin to experience them in our everyday lives. This is what we're learning. We've understood the essence of it is authority. We have authority over the issues of sickness, disease, demonic, wind and waves, natural things, circumstances. We have complete authority over those. We're going to join Him in those, as long as they are not related to people's free will. So, we have to have wisdom about that which we're going to learn. And then as we begin to experience this, it's all for His glory so that we can continue to reflect and share. It's all about what God does, and we get to experience that and enjoy that continually.

For this session, we will explore the keys to experiencing the supernatural. First, we will look at it from the perspective of the person receiving it. What are some of the actions that these people took to put them in a position to experience the supernatural? We will look at the verbs that describe this.

WHAT IS THE PROCESS FOR EXPERIENCING THE SUPERNATURAL?

For each of the following verses, write down the actions (the verbs) that each receiver of the supernatural took to be in a position to receive Christ's supernatural work for them:

LESSON 3:
WHAT ARE THE KEYS TO EXPERIENCING THE SUPERNATURAL?

Matthew 8:1-4:

Jesus Cleanses a Leper

8 When he came down from the mountain, great crowds followed him. ² And behold, a leper[a] came to him and knelt before him, saying, "Lord, if you will, you can make me clean." ³ And Jesus[b] stretched out his hand and touched him, saying, "I will; be clean." And immediately his leprosy was cleansed.⁴ And Jesus said to him, "See that you say nothing to anyone, but go, show yourself to the priest and offer the gift that Moses commanded, for a proof to them."

_____
_____
_____
_____
_____

LESSON 3:
WHAT ARE THE KEYS TO EXPERIENCING THE SUPERNATURAL?

Matthew 8:5-10:

The Faith of a Centurion
5 When he had entered Capernaum, a centurion came forward to him, appealing to him, 6 "Lord, my servant is lying paralyzed at home, suffering terribly." 7 And he said to him, "I will come and heal him." 8 But the centurion replied, "Lord, I am not worthy to have you come under my roof, but only say the word, and my servant will be healed. 9 For I too am a man under authority, with soldiers under me. And I say to one, 'Go,' and he goes, and to another, 'Come,' and he comes, and to my servant,[a] 'Do this,' and he does it." 10 When Jesus heard this, he marveled and said to those who followed him, "Truly, I tell you, with no one in Israel [b] have I found such faith.

_____
_____
_____
_____
_____

Matthew 9:27-31:

Jesus Heals Two Blind Men
27 And as Jesus passed on from there, two blind men followed him, crying aloud, "Have mercy on us, Son of David." 28 When he entered the house, the blind men came to him, and Jesus said to them, "Do you believe that I am able to do this?" They said to him, "Yes, Lord." 29 Then he touched their eyes, saying, "According to your faith be it done to you." 30 And their eyes were opened. And Jesus sternly warned them, "See that no one knows about it." 31 But they went away and spread his fame through all that district.

_____
_____
_____
_____
_____

LESSON 3:
WHAT ARE THE KEYS TO EXPERIENCING THE SUPERNATURAL?

> **Matthew 14:22-29:**
>
> Jesus Walks on the Water
> 22 Immediately he made the disciples get into the boat and go before him to the other side, while he dismissed the crowds. 23 And after he had dismissed the crowds, he went up on the mountain by himself to pray. When evening came, he was there alone, 24 but the boat by this time was a long way[a] from the land,[b] beaten by the waves, for the wind was against them. 25 And in the fourth watch of the night[c] he came to them, walking on the sea. 26 But when the disciples saw him walking on the sea, they were terrified, and said, "It is a ghost!" and they cried out in fear. 27 But immediately Jesus spoke to them, saying, "Take heart; it is I. Do not be afraid."
>
> 28 And Peter answered him, "Lord, if it is you, command me to come to you on the water." 29 He said, "Come." So Peter got out of the boat and walked on the water and came to Jesus.

_____
_____
_____
_____
_____

LESSON 3:
WHAT ARE THE KEYS TO EXPERIENCING THE SUPERNATURAL?

> **Matthew 20:29-34:**
>
> Jesus Heals Two Blind Men
> ²⁹ And as they went out of Jericho, a great crowd followed him. ³⁰ And behold, there were two blind men sitting by the roadside, and when they heard that Jesus was passing by, they cried out, "Lord,[a] have mercy on us, Son of David!" ³¹ The crowd rebuked them, telling them to be silent, but they cried out all the more, "Lord, have mercy on us, Son of David!" ³² And stopping, Jesus called them and said, "What do you want me to do for you?" ³³ They said to him, "Lord, let our eyes be opened."³⁴ And Jesus in pity touched their eyes, and immediately they recovered their sight and followed him.

_____
_____
_____
_____
_____

> **Mark 2:1-5:**
>
> Jesus Heals a Paralytic
> **2** And when he returned to Capernaum after some days, it was reported that he was at home. ² And many were gathered together, so that there was no more room, not even at the door. And he was preaching the word to them. ³ And they came, bringing to him a paralytic carried by four men. ⁴ And when they could not get near him because of the crowd, they removed the roof above him, and when they had made an opening, they let down the bed on which the paralytic lay. ⁵ And when Jesus saw their faith, he said to the paralytic, "Son, your sins are forgiven."

_____
_____
_____
_____
_____

LESSON 3:
WHAT ARE THE KEYS TO EXPERIENCING THE SUPERNATURAL?

> **Mark 2:10-12:**
>
> [10] But that you may know that the Son of Man has authority on earth to forgive sins"—he said to the paralytic— [11] "I say to you, rise, pick up your bed, and go home." [12] And he rose and immediately picked up his bed and went out before them all, so that they were all amazed and glorified God, saying, "We never saw anything like this!"

_____
_____
_____
_____

> **Mark 9:21-26:**
>
> [21] And Jesus asked his father, "How long has this been happening to him?" And he said, "From childhood. [22] And it has often cast him into fire and into water, to destroy him. But if you can do anything, have compassion on us and help us." [23] And Jesus said to him, "'If you can'! All things are possible for one who believes." [24] Immediately the father of the child cried out[a] and said, "I believe; help my unbelief!" [25] And when Jesus saw that a crowd came running together, he rebuked the unclean spirit, saying to it, "You mute and deaf spirit, I command you, come out of him and never enter him again." [26] And after crying out and convulsing him terribly, it came out, and the boy was like a corpse, so that most of them said, "He is dead."

_____
_____
_____
_____

LESSON 3:
WHAT ARE THE KEYS TO EXPERIENCING THE SUPERNATURAL?

> **Mark 11:20-25:**
>
> The Lesson from the Withered Fig Tree
>
> 20 As they passed by in the morning, they saw the fig tree withered away to its roots. 21 And Peter remembered and said to him, "Rabbi, look! The fig tree that you cursed has withered." 22 And Jesus answered them, "Have faith in God. 23 Truly, I say to you, whoever says to this mountain, 'Be taken up and thrown into the sea,' and does not doubt in his heart, but believes that what he says will come to pass, it will be done for him. 24 Therefore I tell you, whatever you ask in prayer, believe that you have received[a] it, and it will be yours. 25 And whenever you stand praying, forgive, if you have anything against anyone, so that your Father also who is in heaven may forgive you your trespasses."[b]

_____
_____
_____
_____
_____

Luke 8:40-44:

Jesus Heals a Woman and Jairus's Daughter

[40] Now when Jesus returned, the crowd welcomed him, for they were all waiting for him. [41] And there came a man named Jairus, who was a ruler of the synagogue. And falling at Jesus' feet, he implored him to come to his house, [42] for he had an only daughter, about twelve years of age, and she was dying.

As Jesus went, the people pressed around him. [43] And there was a woman who had had a discharge of blood for twelve years, and though she had spent all her living on physicians,[a] she could not be healed by anyone. [44] She came up behind him and touched the fringe of his garment, and immediately her discharge of blood ceased.

_____
_____
_____
_____
_____

Luke 18:35-41:

Jesus Heals a Blind Beggar

35 As he drew near to Jericho, a blind man was sitting by the roadside begging. 36 And hearing a crowd going by, he inquired what this meant. 37 They told him, "Jesus of Nazareth is passing by." 38 And he cried out, "Jesus, Son of David, have mercy on me!" 39 And those who were in front rebuked him, telling him to be silent. But he cried out all the more, "Son of David, have mercy on me!" 40 And Jesus stopped and commanded him to be brought to him. And when he came near, he asked him, 41 "What do you want me to do for you?" He said, "Lord, let me recover my sight."

LESSON 4:
HOW DO WE LIMIT HIS SUPERNATURAL WORK?

As we now move into how we can limit God's supernatural work, remember that it's about God's willingness to bear witness to our great salvation, which He tells us not to neglect. Don't ignore this important work of Him doing miracles, miracles, miracles to bear witness to His life. Also remember, as John wrote, that these works of miracles are shared with us so that we might believe, learn, and experience the supernatural ourselves. Again, this is about His authority that He speaks into each of our situations. We're learning to come to Him and receive this, to begin to understand that these works glorify Him; and to then practice this as we go through it. In this next section, we are going to focus on what can prevent or diminish God's supernatural work.

WHAT PREVENTS OR DIMINISHES IT?

For each of these verses, write out what the aspects are of our view/response to the supernatural that actually prevents/diminishes/limits God from performing His desired supernatural acts in our life. Also, why does this affect Him working so much?

> **Matthew 11:20-24:**
>
> Woe to Unrepentant Cities
> [20] Then he began to denounce the cities where most of his mighty works had been done, because they did not repent. [21] "Woe to you, Chorazin! Woe to you, Bethsaida! For if the mighty works done in you had been done in Tyre and Sidon, they would have repented long ago in sackcloth and ashes. [22] But I tell you, it will be more bearable on the day of judgment for Tyre and Sidon than for you. [23] And you, Capernaum, will you be exalted to heaven? You will be brought down to Hades. For if the mighty works done in you had been done in Sodom, it would have remained until this day. [24] But I tell you that it will be more tolerable on the day of judgment for the land of Sodom than for you."

LESSON 4:
HOW DO WE LIMIT HIS SUPERNATURAL WORK?

> **Matthew 13:53-58:**
>
> Jesus Rejected at Nazareth
> [53] And when Jesus had finished these parables, he went away from there, [54] and coming to his hometown he taught them in their synagogue, so that they were astonished, and said, "Where did this man get this wisdom and these mighty works? [55] Is not this the carpenter's son? Is not his mother called Mary? And are not his brothers James and Joseph and Simon and Judas? [56] And are not all his sisters with us? Where then did this man get all these things?" [57] And they took offense at him. But Jesus said to them, "A prophet is not without honor except in his hometown and in his own household." [58] And he did not do many mighty works there, because of their unbelief.

LESSON 4:
HOW DO WE LIMIT HIS SUPERNATURAL WORK?

Mark 3:20-27:

20 Then he went home, and the crowd gathered again, so that they could not even eat. 21 And when his family heard it, they went out to seize him, for they were saying, "He is out of his mind."
Blasphemy Against the Holy Spirit
22 And the scribes who came down from Jerusalem were saying, "He is possessed by Beelzebul," and "by the prince of demons he casts out the demons." 23 And he called them to him and said to them in parables, "How can Satan cast out Satan? 24 If a kingdom is divided against itself, that kingdom cannot stand. 25 And if a house is divided against itself, that house will not be able to stand. 26 And if Satan has risen up against himself and is divided, he cannot stand, but is coming to an end. 27 But no one can enter a strong man's house and plunder his goods, unless he first binds the strong man. Then indeed he may plunder his house.

LESSON 4:
HOW DO WE LIMIT HIS SUPERNATURAL WORK?

> **Mark 5:35-40:**
>
> [35] While he was still speaking, there came from the ruler's house some who said, "Your daughter is dead. Why trouble the Teacher any further?" [36] But overhearing[a] what they said, Jesus said to the ruler of the synagogue, "Do not fear, only believe."[37] And he allowed no one to follow him except Peter and James and John the brother of James. [38] They came to the house of the ruler of the synagogue, and Jesus[b] saw a commotion, people weeping and wailing loudly. [39] And when he had entered, he said to them, "Why are you making a commotion and weeping? The child is not dead but sleeping." [40] And they laughed at him. But he put them all outside and took the child's father and mother and those who were with him and went in where the child was.

_____
_____
_____
_____
_____

LESSON 4:
HOW DO WE LIMIT HIS SUPERNATURAL WORK?

Mark 6:1-6:

Jesus Rejected at Nazareth

6 He went away from there and came to his hometown, and his disciples followed him. ² And on the Sabbath he began to teach in the synagogue, and many who heard him were astonished, saying, "Where did this man get these things? What is the wisdom given to him? How are such mighty works done by his hands? ³ Is not this the carpenter, the son of Mary and brother of James and Joses and Judas and Simon? And are not his sisters here with us?" And they took offense at him. ⁴ And Jesus said to them, "A prophet is not without honor, except in his hometown and among his relatives and in his own household." ⁵ And he could do no mighty work there, except that he laid his hands on a few sick people and healed them. ⁶ And he marveled because of their unbelief.

And he went about among the villages teaching.

LESSON 4:
HOW DO WE LIMIT HIS SUPERNATURAL WORK?

Mark 6:51-52:

[51] And he got into the boat with them, and the wind ceased. And they were utterly astounded, [52] for they did not understand about the loaves, but their hearts were hardened.

Mark 8:1-4:

Jesus Feeds the Four Thousand
8 In those days, when again a great crowd had gathered, and they had nothing to eat, he called his disciples to him and said to them, [2] "I have compassion on the crowd, because they have been with me now three days and have nothing to eat. [3] And if I send them away hungry to their homes, they will faint on the way. And some of them have come from far away." [4] And his disciples answered him, "How can one feed these people with bread here in this desolate place?"

LESSON 4:
HOW DO WE LIMIT HIS SUPERNATURAL WORK?

Mark 8:11-12:

The Pharisees Demand a Sign

[11] The Pharisees came and began to argue with him, seeking from him a sign from heaven to test him. [12] And he sighed deeply in his spirit and said, "Why does this generation seek a sign? Truly, I say to you, no sign will be given to this generation."

_____
_____
_____
_____
_____

Mark 8:13-21:

[13] And he left them, got into the boat again, and went to the other side.

The Leaven of the Pharisees and Herod

[14] Now they had forgotten to bring bread, and they had only one loaf with them in the boat. [15] And he cautioned them, saying, "Watch out; beware of the leaven of the Pharisees and the leaven of Herod."[a] [16] And they began discussing with one another the fact that they had no bread. [17] And Jesus, aware of this, said to them, "Why are you discussing the fact that you have no bread? Do you not yet perceive or understand? Are your hearts hardened? [18] Having eyes do you

LESSON 4:
HOW DO WE LIMIT HIS SUPERNATURAL WORK?

> not see, and having ears do you not hear? And do you not remember? [19] When I broke the five loaves for the five thousand, how many baskets full of broken pieces did you take up?" They said to him, "Twelve." [20] "And the seven for the four thousand, how many baskets full of broken pieces did you take up?" And they said to him, "Seven." [21] And he said to them, "Do you not yet understand?"

_____
_____
_____
_____
_____

WHAT ARE THE KEYS TO EXPERIENCING THE SUPERNATURAL?

As we conclude this session, we will begin looking at the keys to experiencing the supernatural (we also will continue this exploration into the next session). Now that we have learned what prevents or diminishes the supernatural, we can pursue how to experience this in our lives.

LESSON 4:
HOW DO WE LIMIT HIS SUPERNATURAL WORK?

What does this story reveal as the primary basis of the supernatural? How does it really work? What must we fully understand about this if we are going to experience it as a normal part of our lives?

Matthew 8:5-13:

The Faith of a Centurion

[5] When he had entered Capernaum, a centurion came forward to him, appealing to him, [6] "Lord, my servant is lying paralyzed at home, suffering terribly." [7] And he said to him, "I will come and heal him." [8] But the centurion replied, "Lord, I am not worthy to have you come under my roof, but only say the word, and my servant will be healed. [9] For I too am a man under authority, with soldiers under me. And I say to one, 'Go,' and he goes, and to another, 'Come,' and he comes, and to my servant,[a] 'Do this,' and he does it." [10] When Jesus heard this, he marveled and said to those who followed him, "Truly, I tell you, with no one in Israel[b] have I found such faith. [11] I tell you, many will come from east and west and recline at table with Abraham, Isaac, and Jacob in the kingdom of heaven, [12] while the sons of the kingdom will be thrown into the outer darkness. In that place there will be weeping and gnashing of teeth." [13] And to the centurion Jesus said, "Go; let it be done for you as you have believed." And the servant was healed at that very moment.

_____
_____
_____
_____
_____

LESSON 4:
HOW DO WE LIMIT HIS SUPERNATURAL WORK?

1. As you have a problem, an issue, or a circumstance that is troubling, or something is going on that's not healthy, we are to seek Him first and ask Him a simple question: "What do you have to say about this?" From there, you process it together with God and also with your husband, with your wife, with friends, or with your group until you receive understanding and clarity and know exactly what His Word is to you about this.

2. Then, He will ask us: "Do you believe it? Do you have faith now?" Usually, the answer is "not really." So, how do we get to faith? Let's explore this.

    How do the following verses define faith? What is the importance of this definition as established? In verse 3, on what basis was the material (the world) created? What does that mean about your circumstances for which you are seeking supernatural answers?

> **Hebrews 11:1-3:**
>
> By Faith
> **11** Now faith is the assurance of things hoped for, the conviction of things not seen.[2] For by it the people of old received their commendation. [3] By faith we understand that the universe was created by the word of God, so that what is seen was not made out of things that are visible.

_____
_____
_____
_____
_____

LESSON 4:
HOW DO WE LIMIT HIS SUPERNATURAL WORK?

Since faith is required to go to certainty, how do I get to the faith that leads to certainty? From the following verses, what is the process to have faith? How does it work for us?

> **Hebrews 12:1-2:**
>
> Jesus, Founder and Perfecter of Our Faith
> **12** Therefore, since we are surrounded by so great a cloud of witnesses, let us also lay aside every weight, and sin which clings so closely, and let us run with endurance the race that is set before us, ² looking to Jesus, the founder and perfecter of our faith, who for the joy that was set before him endured the cross, despising the shame, and is seated at the right hand of the throne of God.

_____
_____
_____
_____
_____

What is the process for Him to finish His work of taking us (me) to faith? What is our (my) responsibility in this and why?

> **Romans 10:17:**
>
> ¹⁷ So faith comes from hearing, and hearing through the word of Christ.

_____
_____
_____
_____
_____

LESSON 4:
HOW DO WE LIMIT HIS SUPERNATURAL WORK?

What was the key for the woman with a long-term infirmity receiving her healing? What did she do to receive it, and why is that so important for us to receive the supernatural?

> **Matthew 9:18-26:**
>
> A Girl Restored to Life and a Woman Healed
> [18] While he was saying these things to them, behold, a ruler came in and knelt before him, saying, "My daughter has just died, but come and lay your hand on her, and she will live." [19] And Jesus rose and followed him, with his disciples. [20] And behold, a woman who had suffered from a discharge of blood for twelve years came up behind him and touched the fringe of his garment, [21] for she said to herself, "If I only touch his garment, I will be made well." [22] Jesus turned, and seeing her he said, "Take heart, daughter; your faith has made you well." And instantly[a] the woman was made well. [23] And when Jesus came to the ruler's house and saw the flute players and the crowd making a commotion, [24] he said, "Go away, for the girl is not dead but sleeping." And they laughed at him. [25] But when the crowd had been put outside, he went in and took her by the hand, and the girl arose. [26] And the report of this went through all that district.

_____
_____
_____
_____
_____

LESSON 4:
HOW DO WE LIMIT HIS SUPERNATURAL WORK?

What she knew was based upon a truth that she had received and believed. What do all of the following verses reveal about the power in the hem of His garment? What was the truth beneath this, and why was she so sure she would be healed if she could just touch it? Power did go out by faith, and Jesus commended her for this faith. What does this teach us about the process that is important for us?

> **Numbers 15:37-41:**
>
> Tassels on Garments
> 37 The Lord said to Moses, 38 "Speak to the people of Israel, and tell them to make tassels on the corners of their garments throughout their generations, and to put a cord of blue on the tassel of each corner. 39 And it shall be a tassel for you to look at and remember all the commandments of the Lord, to do them, not to follow[a] after your own heart and your own eyes, which you are inclined to whore after. 40 So you shall remember and do all my commandments, and be holy to your God. 41 I am the Lord your God, who brought you out of the land of Egypt to be your God: I am the Lord your God."

_____
_____
_____
_____

LESSON 4:
HOW DO WE LIMIT HIS SUPERNATURAL WORK?

What do the following verses reveal about the power in the hem of His garment? Why is this important for us to understand about His authority for us?

> **Malachi 4:2-3:**
>
> ² But for you who fear my name, the sun of righteousness shall rise with healing in its wings. You shall go out leaping like calves from the stall. ³ And you shall tread down the wicked, for they will be ashes under the soles of your feet, on the day when I act, says the Lord of hosts.

_____
_____
_____
_____
_____

LESSON 4:
HOW DO WE LIMIT HIS SUPERNATURAL WORK?

> **Psalm 36:5-12:**
>
> ⁵ Your steadfast love, O Lord, extends to the heavens,
>   your faithfulness to the clouds.
> ⁶ Your righteousness is like the mountains of God;
>   your judgments are like the great deep;
>   man and beast you save, O Lord.
> ⁷ How precious is your steadfast love, O God!
>   The children of mankind take refuge in the shadow of your wings.
> ⁸ They feast on the abundance of your house,
>   and you give them drink from the river of your delights.
> ⁹ For with you is the fountain of life;
>   in your light do we see light.
> ¹⁰ Oh, continue your steadfast love to those who know you,
>   and your righteousness to the upright of heart!
> ¹¹ Let not the foot of arrogance come upon me,
>   nor the hand of the wicked drive me away.
> ¹² There the evildoers lie fallen;
>   they are thrust down, unable to rise.

_____
_____
_____
_____
_____
_____

LESSON 5:
WHAT IS IMPORTANT IF WE ARE TO EXPERIENCE THE SUPERNATURAL?

God wants to bear witness to this great salvation, and He wants us to pay attention to it. He wants to bear witness with miracles, miracles, miracles, to demonstrate His glory, and He wants to do miracles in all of His children's lives. We've learned the miracles come when we submit to His authority and believe what He speaks. We hear what He has to say as He then takes us to faith, where He asks if we believe. It's His work, not ours. Are we willing to receive it and then are we willing to stay with Him as He gives us the faith to experience His supernatural work? This session continues our exploration of the keys to experiencing the supernatural.

WHAT ARE THE KEYS TO EXPERIENCING THE SUPERNATURAL (CONTINUED)?

From the following verses, write out the principle that Jesus is wanting us to understand about experiencing the supernatural. How does this apply to us personally?

> **Matthew 12:9-14:**
>
> A Man with a Withered Hand
> [9] He went on from there and entered their synagogue. [10] And a man was there with a withered hand. And they asked him, "Is it lawful to heal on the Sabbath?"—so that they might accuse him. [11] He said to them, "Which one of you who has a sheep, if it falls into a pit on the Sabbath, will not take hold of it and lift it out? [12] Of how much more value is a man than a sheep! So it is lawful to do good on the Sabbath." [13] Then he said to the man, "Stretch out your hand." And the man stretched it out, and it was restored, healthy like the other. [14] But the Pharisees went out and conspired against him, how to destroy him.

LESSON 5:
WHAT IS IMPORTANT IF WE ARE TO EXPERIENCE THE SUPERNATURAL?

Matthew 12:22-30:

Blasphemy Against the Holy Spirit

[22] Then a demon-oppressed man who was blind and mute was brought to him, and he healed him, so that the man spoke and saw. [23] And all the people were amazed, and said, "Can this be the Son of David?" [24] But when the Pharisees heard it, they said, "It is only by Beelzebul, the prince of demons, that this man casts out demons." [25] Knowing their thoughts, he said to them, "Every kingdom divided against itself is laid waste, and no city or house divided against itself will stand. [26] And if Satan casts out Satan, he is divided against himself. How then will his kingdom stand? [27] And if I cast out demons by Beelzebul, by whom do your sons cast them out? Therefore they will be your judges. [28] But if it is by the Spirit of God that I cast out demons, then the kingdom of God has come upon you. [29] Or how can someone enter a strong man's house and plunder his goods, unless he first binds the strong man? Then indeed he may plunder his house. [30] Whoever is not with me is against me, and whoever does not gather with me scatters.

LESSON 5:
WHAT IS IMPORTANT IF WE ARE TO EXPERIENCE THE SUPERNATURAL?

Write out how we are to move past the point where we struggle with believing something bigger or different than we have experienced. Since He does not want us to quit, what is important at that moment when we tend to want to quit? How does this work in our personal situations?

> **Matthew 17:14-21:**
>
> Jesus Heals a Boy with a Demon
> [14] And when they came to the crowd, a man came up to him and, kneeling before him, [15] said, "Lord, have mercy on my son, for he has seizures, and he suffers terribly. For often he falls into the fire, and often into the water. [16] And I brought him to your disciples, and they could not heal him." [17] And Jesus answered, "O faithless and twisted generation, how long am I to be with you? How long am I to bear with you? Bring him here to me." [18] And Jesus rebuked the demon,[a] and it[b] came out of him, and the boy was healed instantly.[c] [19] Then the disciples came to Jesus privately and said, "Why could we not cast it out?" [20] He said to them, "Because of your little faith. For truly, I say to you, if you have faith like a grain of mustard seed, you will say to this mountain, 'Move from here to there,' and it will move, and nothing will be impossible for you.[d] [21] [a]However, this kind does not go out except by prayer and fasting."

_____
_____
_____
_____
_____
_____

LESSON 5:
WHAT IS IMPORTANT IF WE ARE TO EXPERIENCE THE SUPERNATURAL?

Write out the key from these verses that guarantees that we will receive what we pray. On what basis do we receive this? Why? How does this work practically in our everyday situations?

> **Matthew 18:18-20:**
>
> [18] Truly, I say to you, whatever you bind on earth shall be bound in heaven, and whatever you loose on earth shall be loosed[a] in heaven. [19] Again I say to you, if two of you agree on earth about anything they ask, it will be done for them by my Father in heaven. [20] For where two or three are gathered in my name, there am I among them."

_____
_____
_____
_____
_____

In the situation where we struggle believing (and as we learned, this will be happening all the time), what are we not to do and what are we to do? Why? What does He promise to do on our behalf to fulfill this request?

> **Mark 9:23-24:**
>
> [23] And Jesus said to him, "'If you can'! All things are possible for one who believes." [24] Immediately the father of the child cried out[a] and said, "I believe; help my unbelief!"

_____
_____
_____
_____
_____

LESSON 5:
WHAT IS IMPORTANT IF WE ARE TO EXPERIENCE THE SUPERNATURAL?

Mark 11:20-25:

The Lesson from the Withered Fig Tree
[20] As they passed by in the morning, they saw the fig tree withered away to its roots. [21] And Peter remembered and said to him, "Rabbi, look! The fig tree that you cursed has withered." [22] And Jesus answered them, "Have faith in God. [23] Truly, I say to you, whoever says to this mountain, 'Be taken up and thrown into the sea,' and does not doubt in his heart, but believes that what he says will come to pass, it will be done for him. [24] Therefore I tell you, whatever you ask in prayer, believe that you have received[a] it, and it will be yours. [25] And whenever you stand praying, forgive, if you have anything against anyone, so that your Father also who is in heaven may forgive you your trespasses."[b]

Luke 9:1-2:

Jesus Sends Out the Twelve Apostles
9 And he called the twelve together and gave them power and authority over all demons and to cure diseases, [2] and he sent them out to proclaim the kingdom of God and to heal.

LESSON 5:
WHAT IS IMPORTANT IF WE ARE TO EXPERIENCE THE SUPERNATURAL?

> **Luke 11:14-23:**
>
> Jesus and Beelzebul
>
> [14] Now he was casting out a demon that was mute. When the demon had gone out, the mute man spoke, and the people marveled. [15] But some of them said, "He casts out demons by Beelzebul, the prince of demons," [16] while others, to test him, kept seeking from him a sign from heaven. [17] But he, knowing their thoughts, said to them, "Every kingdom divided against itself is laid waste, and a divided household falls. [18] And if Satan also is divided against himself, how will his kingdom stand? For you say that I cast out demons by Beelzebul. [19] And if I cast out demons by Beelzebul, by whom do your sons cast them out? Therefore they will be your judges. [20] But if it is by the finger of God that I cast out demons, then the kingdom of God has come upon you. [21] When a strong man, fully armed, guards his own palace, his goods are safe; [22] but when one stronger than he attacks him and overcomes him, he takes away his armor in which he trusted and divides his spoil. [23] Whoever is not with me is against me, and whoever does not gather with me scatters.

_____
_____
_____
_____
_____

LESSON 5:
WHAT IS IMPORTANT IF WE ARE TO EXPERIENCE THE SUPERNATURAL?

Luke 17:11-19:

Jesus Cleanses Ten Lepers

11 On the way to Jerusalem he was passing along between Samaria and Galilee. 12 And as he entered a village, he was met by ten lepers,[a] who stood at a distance 13 and lifted up their voices, saying, "Jesus, Master, have mercy on us." 14 When he saw them he said to them, "Go and show yourselves to the priests." And as they went they were cleansed. 15 Then one of them, when he saw that he was healed, turned back, praising God with a loud voice; 16 and he fell on his face at Jesus' feet, giving him thanks. Now he was a Samaritan. 17 Then Jesus answered, "Were not ten cleansed? Where are the nine? 18 Was no one found to return and give praise to God except this foreigner?" 19 And he said to him, "Rise and go your way; your faith has made you well."[b]

LESSON 5:
WHAT IS IMPORTANT IF WE ARE TO EXPERIENCE THE SUPERNATURAL?

John 5:16-23; 30:

[16] And this was why the Jews were persecuting Jesus, because he was doing these things on the Sabbath. [17] But Jesus answered them, "My Father is working until now, and I am working."

Jesus Is Equal with God
[18] This was why the Jews were seeking all the more to kill him, because not only was he breaking the Sabbath, but he was even calling God his own Father, making himself equal with God.

The Authority of the Son
[19] So Jesus said to them, "Truly, truly, I say to you, the Son can do nothing of his own accord, but only what he sees the Father doing. For whatever the Father[a] does, that the Son does likewise. [20] For the Father loves the Son and shows him all that he himself is doing. And greater works than these will he show him, so that you may marvel. [21] For as the Father raises the dead and gives them life, so also the Son gives life to whom he will. [22] For the Father judges no one, but has given all judgment to the Son, [23] that all may honor the Son, just as they honor the Father. Whoever does not honor the Son does not honor the Father who sent him.

Witnesses to Jesus
[30] "I can do nothing on my own. As I hear, I judge, and my judgment is just, because I seek not my own will but the will of him who sent me.

_____
_____
_____
_____
_____

LESSON 5:
WHAT IS IMPORTANT IF WE ARE TO EXPERIENCE THE SUPERNATURAL?

John 14:7-14:

7 If you had known me, you would have known my Father also.[a] From now on you do know him and have seen him."

8 Philip said to him, "Lord, show us the Father, and it is enough for us." 9 Jesus said to him, "Have I been with you so long, and you still do not know me, Philip? Whoever has seen me has seen the Father. How can you say, 'Show us the Father'? 10 Do you not believe that I am in the Father and the Father is in me? The words that I say to you I do not speak on my own authority, but the Father who dwells in me does his works. 11 Believe me that I am in the Father and the Father is in me, or else believe on account of the works themselves.

12 "Truly, truly, I say to you, whoever believes in me will also do the works that I do; and greater works than these will he do, because I am going to the Father. 13 Whatever you ask in my name, this I will do, that the Father may be glorified in the Son. 14 If you ask me[b] anything in my name, I will do it.

_____

_____

_____

_____

_____

LESSON 5:
WHAT IS IMPORTANT IF WE ARE TO EXPERIENCE THE SUPERNATURAL?

John 15:5-8:

⁵ I am the vine; you are the branches. Whoever abides in me and I in him, he it is that bears much fruit, for apart from me you can do nothing. ⁶ If anyone does not abide in me he is thrown away like a branch and withers; and the branches are gathered, thrown into the fire, and burned. ⁷ If you abide in me, and my words abide in you, ask whatever you wish, and it will be done for you. ⁸ By this my Father is glorified, that you bear much fruit and so prove to be my disciples.

_____
_____
_____
_____

Matthew 9:27-31:

Jesus Heals Two Blind Men
²⁷ And as Jesus passed on from there, two blind men followed him, crying aloud, "Have mercy on us, Son of David." ²⁸ When he entered the house, the blind men came to him, and Jesus said to them, "Do you believe that I am able to do this?" They said to him, "Yes, Lord." ²⁹ Then he touched their eyes, saying, "According to your faith be it done to you." ³⁰ And their eyes were opened. And Jesus sternly warned them, "See that no one knows about it." ³¹ But they went away and spread his fame through all that district.

_____
_____
_____
_____

LESSON 5:
WHAT IS IMPORTANT IF WE ARE TO EXPERIENCE THE SUPERNATURAL?

Matthew 15:21-28:

The Faith of a Canaanite Woman

[21] And Jesus went away from there and withdrew to the district of Tyre and Sidon. [22] And behold, a Canaanite woman from that region came out and was crying, "Have mercy on me, O Lord, Son of David; my daughter is severely oppressed by a demon." [23] But he did not answer her a word. And his disciples came and begged him, saying, "Send her away, for she is crying out after us." [24] He answered, "I was sent only to the lost sheep of the house of Israel." [25] But she came and knelt before him, saying, "Lord, help me." [26] And he answered, "It is not right to take the children's bread and throw it to the dogs." [27] She said, "Yes, Lord, yet even the dogs eat the crumbs that fall from their masters' table." [28] Then Jesus answered her, "O woman, great is your faith! Be it done for you as you desire." And her daughter was healed instantly.[a]

_____
_____
_____
_____

LESSON 5:
WHAT IS IMPORTANT IF WE ARE TO EXPERIENCE THE SUPERNATURAL?

> **Matthew 15:32-39:**
>
> Jesus Feeds the Four Thousand
>
> 32 Then Jesus called his disciples to him and said, "I have compassion on the crowd because they have been with me now three days and have nothing to eat. And I am unwilling to send them away hungry, lest they faint on the way." 33 And the disciples said to him, "Where are we to get enough bread in such a desolate place to feed so great a crowd?" 34 And Jesus said to them, "How many loaves do you have?" They said, "Seven, and a few small fish." 35 And directing the crowd to sit down on the ground, 36 he took the seven loaves and the fish, and having given thanks he broke them and gave them to the disciples, and the disciples gave them to the crowds. 37 And they all ate and were satisfied. And they took up seven baskets full of the broken pieces left over. 38 Those who ate were four thousand men, besides women and children. 39 And after sending away the crowds, he got into the boat and went to the region of Magadan.

_____
_____
_____
_____
_____
_____

LESSON 6:
AS WE EXPERIENCE THE SUPERNATURAL, WE ALSO ARE CALLED TO HELP OTHERS EXPERIENCE THE SUPERNATURAL

As we go into our sixth and final session, we've learned about the life of the supernatural. God wants to bear witness to this great salvation, and we are not to neglect this by our unwillingness to come and learn it. Don't say *no* to it, but instead say *yes*. In that, as John wrote, we could experience the miracles, and believe in the miracles, and live out the miracles. We've learned a lot about authority, hearing what He has to say, believing what He has to say, declaring what He has to say, and then beginning to experience what He has to say, all of which prepare us to recognize what that looks like in our real, everyday life. As we experience it, we will start to teach others that experiencing the supernatural is possible for them, too. We are called to receive and give it away.

WE ARE CALLED TO RECEIVE AND GIVE IT AWAY. (COVENANT)

Write out for each of the following verses in what way are we called to give away to, teach others how to experience the Supernatural?

Genesis 12:1-3:

The Call of Abram

12 Now the Lord said[a] to Abram, "Go from your country[b] and your kindred and your father's house to the land that I will show you. ² And I will make of you a great nation, and I will bless you and make your name great, so that you will be a blessing. ³ I will bless those who bless you, and him who dishonors you I will curse, and in you all the families of the earth shall be blessed."[c]

_____
_____
_____
_____
_____
_____

LESSON 6:
AS WE EXPERIENCE THE SUPERNATURAL, WE ALSO ARE CALLED TO HELP OTHERS EXPERIENCE THE SUPERNATURAL

> **Ephesians 1:15-21:**
>
> Thanksgiving and Prayer
>
> [15] For this reason, because I have heard of your faith in the Lord Jesus and your love[a] toward all the saints, [16] I do not cease to give thanks for you, remembering you in my prayers, [17] that the God of our Lord Jesus Christ, the Father of glory, may give you the Spirit of wisdom and of revelation in the knowledge of him, [18] having the eyes of your hearts enlightened, that you may know what is the hope to which he has called you, what are the riches of his glorious inheritance in the saints, [19] and what is the immeasurable greatness of his power toward us who believe, according to the working of his great might [20] that he worked in Christ when he raised him from the dead and seated him at his right hand in the heavenly places, [21] far above all rule and authority and power and dominion, and above every name that is named, not only in this age but also in the one to come.

_____
_____
_____
_____
_____

LESSON 6:
AS WE EXPERIENCE THE SUPERNATURAL, WE ALSO ARE CALLED TO HELP OTHERS EXPERIENCE THE SUPERNATURAL

Ephesians 3:15-21:

15 from whom every family[a] in heaven and on earth is named, 16 that according to the riches of his glory he may grant you to be strengthened with power through his Spirit in your inner being, 17 so that Christ may dwell in your hearts through faith—that you, being rooted and grounded in love, 18 may have strength to comprehend with all the saints what is the breadth and length and height and depth, 19 and to know the love of Christ that surpasses knowledge, that you may be filled with all the fullness of God.
20 Now to him who is able to do far more abundantly than all that we ask or think, according to the power at work within us, 21 to him be glory in the church and in Christ Jesus throughout all generations, forever and ever. Amen.

_____
_____
_____
_____
_____

Matthew 10:5-8:

Jesus Sends Out the Twelve Apostles
5 These twelve Jesus sent out, instructing them, "Go nowhere among the Gentiles and enter no town of the Samaritans, 6 but go rather to the lost sheep of the house of Israel. 7 And proclaim as you go, saying, 'The kingdom of heaven is at hand.'[a] 8 Heal the sick, raise the dead, cleanse lepers,[b] cast out demons. You received without paying; give without pay.

_____
_____
_____
_____
_____

LESSON 6:
AS WE EXPERIENCE THE SUPERNATURAL, WE ALSO ARE CALLED TO HELP OTHERS EXPERIENCE THE SUPERNATURAL

Matthew 10:24-31:

24 "A disciple is not above his teacher, nor a servant[a] above his master. 25 It is enough for the disciple to be like his teacher, and the servant like his master. If they have called the master of the house Beelzebul, how much more will they malign[b] those of his household.

Have No Fear
26 "So have no fear of them, for nothing is covered that will not be revealed, or hidden that will not be known. 27 What I tell you in the dark, say in the light, and what you hear whispered, proclaim on the housetops.28 And do not fear those who kill the body but cannot kill the soul. Rather fear him who can destroy both soul and body in hell.[c]29 Are not two sparrows sold for a penny?[d]And not one of them will fall to the ground apart from your Father. 30 But even the hairs of your head are all numbered. 31 Fear not, therefore; you are of more value than many sparrows.

_____
_____
_____
_____
_____

LESSON 6:
AS WE EXPERIENCE THE SUPERNATURAL, WE ALSO ARE CALLED TO HELP OTHERS EXPERIENCE THE SUPERNATURAL

Matthew 14:13-21:

Jesus Feeds the Five Thousand

13 Now when Jesus heard this, he withdrew from there in a boat to a desolate place by himself. But when the crowds heard it, they followed him on foot from the towns. 14 When he went ashore, he saw a great crowd, and he had compassion on them and healed their sick. 15 Now when it was evening, the disciples came to him and said, "This is a desolate place, and the day is now over; send the crowds away to go into the villages and buy food for themselves." 16 But Jesus said, "They need not go away; you give them something to eat." 17 They said to him, "We have only five loaves here and two fish." 18 And he said, "Bring them here to me." 19 Then he ordered the crowds to sit down on the grass, and taking the five loaves and the two fish, he looked up to heaven and said a blessing. Then he broke the loaves and gave them to the disciples, and the disciples gave them to the crowds. 20 And they all ate and were satisfied. And they took up twelve baskets full of the broken pieces left over. 21 And those who ate were about five thousand men, besides women and children.

_____
_____
_____
_____

Luke 10:1-20:

Jesus Sends Out the Seventy-Two

10 After this the Lord appointed seventy-two[a] others and sent them on ahead of him, two by two, into every town and place where he himself was about to go. 2 And he said to them, "The harvest is plentiful, but the laborers are few. Therefore, pray earnestly to the Lord of the harvest to send out laborers into his harvest. 3 Go your way; behold, I am sending you out as lambs in the midst of wolves. 4 Carry no moneybag, no knapsack, no sandals, and greet no one on the road. 5 Whatever house you enter, first say, 'Peace be to this house!' 6 And if a

LESSON 6:
AS WE EXPERIENCE THE SUPERNATURAL, WE ALSO ARE CALLED TO HELP OTHERS EXPERIENCE THE SUPERNATURAL

son of peace is there, your peace will rest upon him. But if not, it will return to you. [7] And remain in the same house, eating and drinking what they provide, for the laborer deserves his wages. Do not go from house to house. [8] Whenever you enter a town and they receive you, eat what is set before you. [9] Heal the sick in it and say to them, 'The kingdom of God has come near to you.' [10] But whenever you enter a town and they do not receive you, go into its streets and say, [11] 'Even the dust of your town that clings to our feet we wipe off against you. Nevertheless, know this, that the kingdom of God has come near.' [12] I tell you, it will be more bearable on that day for Sodom than for that town.

Woe to Unrepentant Cities
[13] "Woe to you, Chorazin! Woe to you, Bethsaida! For if the mighty works done in you had been done in Tyre and Sidon, they would have repented long ago, sitting in sackcloth and ashes. [14] But it will be more bearable in the judgment for Tyre and Sidon than for you. [15] And you, Capernaum, will you be exalted to heaven? You shall be brought down to Hades.

[16] "The one who hears you hears me, and the one who rejects you rejects me, and the one who rejects me rejects him who sent me."

The Return of the Seventy-Two
[17] The seventy-two returned with joy, saying, "Lord, even the demons are subject to us in your name!" [18] And he said to them, "I saw Satan fall like lightning from heaven. [19] Behold, I have given you authority to tread on serpents and scorpions, and over all the power of the enemy, and nothing shall hurt you. [20] Nevertheless, do not rejoice in this, that the spirits are subject to you, but rejoice that your names are written in heaven."

_____
_____
_____
_____
_____

LESSON 6:
AS WE EXPERIENCE THE SUPERNATURAL, WE ALSO ARE CALLED TO HELP OTHERS EXPERIENCE THE SUPERNATURAL

CONCLUSION:

Remember we started our course with these verses:

Matthew 28:16-20:

The Great Commission

16 Now the eleven disciples went to Galilee, to the mountain to which Jesus had directed them. 17 And when they saw him they worshiped him, but some doubted. 18 And Jesus came and said to them, "All authority in heaven and on earth has been given to me. 19 Go therefore and make disciples of all nations, baptizing them in[a] the name of the Father and of the Son and of the Holy Spirit, 20 teaching them to observe all that I have commanded you. And behold, I am with you always, to the end of the age."

Hebrews 2:1-4:

Warning Against Neglecting Salvation

2 Therefore we must pay much closer attention to what we have heard, lest we drift away from it. 2 For since the message declared by angels proved to be reliable, and every transgression or disobedience received a just retribution, 3 how shall we escape if we neglect such a great salvation? It was declared at first by the Lord, and it was attested to us by those who heard, 4 while God also bore witness by signs and wonders and various miracles and by gifts of the Holy Spirit distributed according to his will.

John 14:12-14:

12 "Truly, truly, I say to you, whoever believes in me will also do the works that I do; and greater works than these will he do, because I am going to the Father. 13 Whatever you ask in my name, this I will do, that the Father may be glorified in the Son. 14 If you ask me[a] anything in my name, I will do it.

History of Abide Ministries

In the 1990s, Rich and Linda Case received a call from God to dig into what it means to truly live in the Spirit.

In the 1990s, Rich and Linda Case received a call from God to dig into what it means to truly live in the Spirit. They had been believers for most of their lives and regularly attended church and Bible studies, but began to realize that, despite knowing the Bible intellectually, their personal experiences seemed disconnected from the promises and truths found in scripture. As they then learned these essential truths through their abiding and hearing God's voice — and began to see the grand life play out in their lives God called them to give that knowledge away. In 2001, God initiated the ABIDE ministry at a retreat with friends in Austria, and through their personal experience of this abiding life, their friends noticed the change in their lives and inquired if Rich and Linda could host a similar retreat the following year. This was repeated three years in a row, and then God called them to host weekend retreats in their home in Colorado.

Through the formal development of the truths revealed by God with Abiding and additional electives, they founded All for Jesus — Living Waters Ministries, now Abide Ministries — and have seen it grow exponentially since then, with 24+ retreat leaders all over the world, 29 online courses, eight books on various aspects of living life with Christ, and a daily podcast. Rich and Linda have also worked with various churches to strengthening them with the truths of an abiding life in Christ, and seeing Christ bring reconciliation and new vision to desperate situations.

Their heart is to bring the truths and promises of God to as many people as possible, showing everyone that when you abide in Christ and seek Him daily, your life can be completely and utterly transformed — enabling you to experience the grand life promised by God.

Vision

At our core, we believe in walking along God's path and connecting to the vine (abiding). As we walk in unity with others and understand God's Word as the truth, we are sure to experience His promised grand life and thus, willingly accept God's will as our chosen path.

Mission

1. Live out and invite everyone to experience the grand, spectacular, abundant life by hearing God's voice.
2. Share God's majesty, a close relationship with us as he yearns for our restoration.
3. God is majestic, grand and pure goodness, so that we can experience His nature in real life.
4. Communicate to everyone, irrespective of their condition, that all are meant to experience God's Divine Life (grand, majestic), by receiving His personal plan for us.
5. God delivers this life for us in a SUPERNATURAL way, transcending human comprehension, and thus, becoming normal in our life.
6. Teach that personal truths are revealed to us by God, grounded on His word – the embodiment of Truth.
7. Recognize that abiding in Christ changes our life in tangible, real ways, and is not just learning about or studying this life.
8. Teach that as we abide in Christ, we learn to understand and amp; follow God's will for our lives, as He leads us personally into His grand, Divine plan for us. His personal plan calls us into His bigger story with our best interest at heart (blessed to bless others).

Statement of Non-Profit Status

Abide Ministries is a not-for-profit 501(c)3 organization that has been fully funded by our founders, leaders and retreat participants since its inception.

Tax-ID number: 27-1731819

Testimonies

"If I'm not abiding, I feel like I'm dying. Abiding is living…It's powerful to know that you have God's perspective on something."

 Steve

"This was the first time that I understood what people meant by God's living Word. And I've been a Christian for a lot of years, but this was the first time it really came alive for me and I really could experience that."

 Dan

"It doesn't matter where you are at in your walk. If you just got saved yesterday or if you've been a 20+ year believer like i have, learning how to hear God's voice and learning His will is just as important in day one as it is in day 3,426. You wanna hear God's will and this course has helped me hear Him more clearly."

 Bob

"Abiding turned out to be the most transformational thing I've ever had since salvation in my Christian walk and in our marriage, and it's just been amazing. God has a path for us and He is there and He's showing it to us."

 Heath

"Before, in my quiet time, it was more of a checklist thing for me to do in the morning, and, honestly, some mornings it was the thing that went if I was busy, and some days it didn't even happen. Now, it's become so personal to me and the time flies by in the morning and God speaks so directly to me and I just never felt that way on a daily basis before. That has been life-altering for me."

 Rebecca

"I heard about people living in peace, I heard about people living in joy, and realizing all kinds of things around them are happening. And then we realize, wait a minute, we're there, we have peace beyond understanding."

 Brad

Giving to the Ministry

Have you experienced abundant blessing from your time with Abide Ministries?

Pay it forward by donating at **abideministries.com/donate** and help us support others in learning how to seek Christ and abide in Him! We appreciate your desire to help us share the Abundant Life with the rest of the world.

Learn More at
abideministries.com

Podcast

Escape the chaos and uncertainty of the world with our podcast, ***"Come and See, Finding Truth in a World of Chaos,"*** available on YouTube, Apple Podcasts, and Spotify.

CHANNEL PLAYLIST PAGE

Tune in five days a week as our hosts, Rich Case and Kathy Rocconi, dive into the scriptures and discuss what it looks like to live an abiding life with Christ. Join us as we seek God's truth in a world of turmoil and darkness.

Online Courses

Abide Ministries online courses uncover life-changing biblical truths, with practical application and wisdom. Our courses are joyful and life-giving and are perfect for small groups as well as individuals.

Each course has an accompanying workbook. Join us as we learn about biblical topics like Hearing God's Voice, Discerning God's Will, the Covenant, Living in Forgiveness, Living in the Kingdom of God, Living in the Supernatural, Christ, Clutter and the Calendar, Living the Grand Life, and many, many more.

 **COURSES**

Abide
Retreats

Learn more at
abideministries.com

> Do you have friends or a small group that you would like to experience what you just experienced?

Would you be interested in attending another retreat, which we call electives to go deeper in your walk with God?

See the various options on our website.
The topics for retreats and courses are the same.

RETREATS	COURSES	STORE

www.ingramcontent.com/pod-product-compliance
Lightning Source LLC
Chambersburg PA
CBHW051258110526
44589CB00025B/2869